The Independent Investigator III

The
INDEPENDENT
Investigator III

Tahirih Lemon

SACRED
Square
Publishing

Published by Sacred Square Publishing Australia
sacredsquarepublishing.com
info@sacredsquarepublishing.com

First published 2022

© Text — Tahirih Lemon, 2022
© Illustrations — Gerald Abol, 2022

The moral right of the author has been asserted.

A catalogue record for this
book is available from the
National Library of Australia

ISBN: 978 0 6485851 5 2 (pbk)

Cover design by Leisa J Creative Design
Typeset by Helen Christie, Blue Wren Books
Illustrations by Gerald Abol
Printed in Australia

Dedication

I would like to dedicate this book to all the junior youth who provided comments and feedback regarding the selection of questions.

Contents

Introduction

This book contains the answers to a whole new range of questions asked by young people just like yourself. It is the third and last book in this series. It is very important that you independently investigate spiritual truth for yourself. One of the principles of the Baha'i Faith is the independent investigation of truth.

It is important that you decide for yourself what is true and just. This is highlighted by the following words of Baha'u'llah, the Founder of the Baha'i Faith:

"O Son of Spirit!

The best beloved of all things in My sight is Justice; turn not away therefrom if thou desirest Me and neglect it not that I may confide in thee. By its aid thou shalt see with thine own eyes and not through the knowledge of thy neighbour. Ponder this in thy heart; how it behooveth thee to be. Verily justice is My gift to thee and the sign of My loving-kindness. Set it then before thine eyes." (*Hidden Words in Arabic*, No. 2)

Keep investigating and continue to seek answers to your questions.

CHAPTER ONE

- The soul
- The body
- The Afterlife

How is the soul connected to the body?

Many people believe their soul is inside their body. Interestingly, your soul never actually enters your body, but rather it is connected to your body while living in this physical world. 'Abdu'l-Bahá explains the connection between your soul and body, and states:

> "... the rational soul, meaning the human spirit, does not descend into the body — that is to say, it does not enter it, for descent and entrance are characteristics of bodies, and the rational soul is exempt from this. The spirit never entered this body, so in quitting it, it will not be in need of an abiding-place: no, the spirit is connected with the body, as this light is with the mirror. When the mirror is clear and perfect, the light of the lamp will be apparent in it, and when the mirror becomes covered with dust or breaks, the light will disappear.
>
> The rational soul — that is to say, the human spirit — has neither entered this body nor existed through it; so after the disintegration of the composition of the body, how should it be in need of a substance through which it may exist? On the contrary, the rational soul is the substance through which the body exists. The personality of the rational soul is from its beginning; it is not due to the instrumentality of the body, but the state and the personality of the rational soul may be strengthened in this world; it will make progress and will attain to the degrees of perfection, or it will remain in the lowest abyss of ignorance, veiled and deprived from beholding the signs of God." (*Some Answered Questions*, pp. 239–240)

'Abdu'l-Bahá describes the soul as a link between the body and spirit. He describes how the soul operates through the body in the following quotes:

> "It receives bounties and virtues from the spirit and gives them to the body just as the outward senses carry to the inward senses what they receive from the outer world in order that

it may remain deposited in the memory and may be made serviceable by man through his power." (*Mahmúd's Diary*, p. 27)

"The spirit of man has two means of action. Sometimes it acts through an **intermediary**. For instance, the spirit of man sees through the intermediary of the eye, hears through the ear, walks with the help of the legs and smells with the nose.

In order to seize the actions of the rational soul, we need the mediation of the body; but the soul can act directly without this intermediary. Thus, when we sleep the soul sees without the help of the eyes. The auditory nerves are inactive, but the soul hears. Our members are in response, but the soul is in movement. Our body is the room, our soul is travelling through all horizons. It is clear, therefore, that the soul evolves with and without the intervention of the material body.

The soul acts in the physical world with the help of the body. When it is freed from the body it acts without an intermediary." (*Divine Philosophy*, pp. 126–28)

How does our soul communicate with our brain?

The brain is the central control system of the body. Its job is to receive, store and transmit messages. The mind interacts with three components: the brain, the soul's mental powers of the imagination, thought, understanding, memory, and the energising force of the human spirit. This is not yet recognised by the medical profession nor psychology.

At present science believes our brain is where our thoughts, understanding and creativity originates from, but in fact they are properties of our soul. 'Abdu'l-Bahá, explains this in the following quotes:

> "Now regarding the question whether the faculties of the mind and the human soul are one and the same. These faculties are the inherent properties of the soul, such as the power of imagination, of thought, of understanding, powers that are the essential requisites of the reality of man, even as the solar ray is the inherent property of the sun. The temple of man is like unto a mirror, his soul is as the sun, and his mental faculties even as the rays that **emanate** from that source of light. The ray may cease to fall upon the mirror, but it can in no wise be dissociated from the sun." (*Tablet to Auguste Forel*, pp. 8–9)

> "As outer circumstances are communicated to the soul by eyes, ears, and brain of a man so does the soul communicate its desires and purposes through the brain to the hands and tongue of the physical body, thereby expressing itself. The spirit in the soul is the very essence of life." (*Paris Talks*, p. 86)

Does dementia stop a person's spiritual development?

Dementia is the loss of a person's ability to think, remember and reason to such an extent that it interferes with the person's daily life and activities. Dementia is a disorder that affects the brain, and it is not one specific disease. A person is diagnosed with dementia every 3 seconds in the world. It is estimated that in 2020, 55 million people around the world were living with dementia and this number will double every 20 years.

Dementia is not a normal part of getting older. It is a brain disease that generally occurs after the age 65. There is currently no cure. Despite these sobering statistics it is reassuring to know our loved ones afflicted with dementia are never truly lost to us.

'Abdu'l-Bahá reassures us that no disease or illness ever affects our soul. This is highlighted in the following quotes:

> "The connection of the spirit with the body is like that of the sun with mirror. Briefly, the human spirit is in one condition. It neither becomes ill from the disease of the body nor cured by its health; it does not become sick, nor weak, nor miserable, nor poor, nor light, nor small — that is to say, it will not be injured because of the infirmities of the body, and no effect will be visible even if the body becomes weak, or if the hands and feet and tongue be cut off, or if it loses the power of hearing or sight." (*Some Answered Questions*, p. 229)

> "The mind is **circumscribed**, the soul is limitless. It is by the aid of such senses as those of sight, hearing, taste, smell and touch, that the mind comprehendeth, whereas, the soul is free from all agencies. The soul as thou observes, whether it be in sleep or waking, is in motion and ever active. Possibly it may, whilst in a dream, unravel an intricate problem, incapable of solution in the waking state." (*Tablet to Auguste Forel*, pp. 8–9)

Tahirih Lemon

Therefore, from the above quotes it is apparent dementia does not stop a person's spiritual development. Continue to pray for them and with them.

Does everyone have intuition?

Intuition sometimes referred to as our 'sixth sense', or the 'third eye' is a 'feeling in your gut' or an 'inner voice' of knowing something is right or wrong instinctively. 'Abdu'l-Bahá explains it is our spirit which advises and decides upon matters. He states:

> "When you wish to reflect upon or consider a matter, you consult something within you. You say, shall I do it, or shall I not do it? It is better to make this journey or abandon it? Whom do you consult? Who is within you deciding this question? Surely there is a distinct power, an intelligent ego. Were it not distinct from your ego, you would not be consulting it. It is greater than the faculty of thought. It is your spirit which teaches you, which advises and decides upon matters." (*The Promulgation of Universal Peace*, p. 243)

> "The Word of God is the storehouse of all good, all power and all wisdom ... It awakens within us that brilliant intuition which makes us independent of all tuition, and endows us with an all-embracing power of spiritual understanding." (*Bahá'í Scriptures*, p. 439)

Shoghi Effendi responded to an individual's question about relying on our intuition to guide us, and states:

> "With regard to your question as to the value of intuition as a source of guidance for the individual: implicit faith in our intuitive powers is unwise, but through daily prayer and sustained effort one can discover, though not always and fully, God's will intuitively. Under no circumstances, however, can a person be absolutely certain that he is recognising God's will, through the exercise of his intuition. It often happens that the latter results in completely misrepresenting the truth, and thus becomes a source of error rather than guidance." (From a letter written on behalf of Shoghi Effendi to an individual believer, dated 29 October 1938.)

'Abdu'l-Bahá elaborates further and acknowledges all human standards of judgement are faulty. He explains:

"The fourth criterion I have named is inspiration through which it is claimed the reality of knowledge is attainable. What is inspiration? It is the influx of the human heart. But what are satanic **promptings** which afflict mankind? They are the influx of the heart also. How shall we differentiate between them? The questions arises, How shall we know whether we are following inspiration from God or satanic promptings of the human soul? Briefly, the point is that in the human material world of phenomena these four are the only existing criterions or avenues of knowledge, and all of them are faulty and unreliable. What then remains? How shall we attain the reality of the knowledge? By the breaths and promptings of the Holy Spirit which is light and knowledge itself. Through it the human mind is quickened and fortified into true conclusions and perfect knowledge. This is conclusive argument showing that all available human criterions are erroneous and defective, but the divine standard of knowledge is infallible. Therefore man is not justified in saying 'I know because I perceive through my sense', or 'I know because it is proved through my faculty of reason'; or 'I know because it is according to tradition and interpretation of the holy book'; or 'I know because I am inspired.' All human standard of judgment is faulty, finite." (*The Promulgation of Universal Peace*, p. 22)

Is there such thing as a soul mate?

There are several definitions and criteria about how to find your soul mate. Basically, a soul mate is your perfect match, in every way. The person you are destined to be with. When asked by an individual about the existence of a soul mate, Shoghi Effendi explains:

> "There is no teaching in the Bahá'í Faith that 'soul mates' exist. What is meant is that marriage should lead to a profound friendship of spirit, which will endure in the next world, where there is no sex, and no giving and taking in marriage; just the way we should establish with our parents, our children, our brothers and sisters and friends a deep spiritual bond which will be ever-lasting, and not merely physical bonds of human relationship." (*Lights of Guidance*, p. 207)

Can the bodies of Bahá'ís be embalmed?

Embalming is a process used to delay the decomposition of a corpse for a little while longer and to give the appearance of 'looking alive' for example when there is an open casket funeral. Embalming involves the draining of the blood, and gases are released by making small incisions. Chemicals are then pumped into the body through the circulatory system.

Discussing whether Bahá'í should be embalmed as part of the preparation of their body for their burial, a letter written to an individual on behalf of Shoghi Effendi states:

"Regarding the questions which you ask, concerning Bahá'í burials ..., etc. At the present time, the Guardian is not stressing these matters, as their establishment might divert attention to the supreme tasks we have before us. However, the answers are as follows: Under the Bahá'í teachings it seems clear that the body is not to be embalmed. The burial should take place within an hour's travel time from the place of death. The preparation for the body for burial is a careful washing, and placing in a shroud of white cloth, silk preferably. There is nothing in the teachings with regard to turning the body over to scientific institutions for scientific research, and therefore the individual may do as he wishes, until such a time as the Universal House of Justice may legislate on this matter, if they ever do. The practice in the Orient, is to bury the person within 24 hours of the time of death; sometimes even sooner; although there is no provision in the teachings as to the time limit." (*Lights of Guidance*, p. 195)

Therefore, Bahá'ís should not have their bodies embalmed. The reality is decomposition is a natural and inevitable process.

Can a Bahá'í donate their body to science?

People who decide to donate their body to science view this act as their contribution to society once they have died. Body donations are usually organised through a university or medical research facility. These donations contribute to the training of future doctors, nurses, specialists, and health professionals. Bodies may be stored for a fortnight up to a few years. The university or facility generally cover the cost of the burial or cremation. Donated bodies are to always be treated with dignity and respect.

With regards to Bahá'ís donating their body to science Shoghi Effendi wrote to an individual believer:

> "There is nothing in the Teachings against leaving our bodies to medical science. The only thing we should **stipulate** is that we do not wish to be cremated, as it is against our Bahá'í Laws.
>
> As many people make arrangements to leave their bodies to medical science for investigation, he suggests that you inquire, either through some lawyer friend or through some hospital, how you could do this, and then make the necessary provision in your Will, stipulating that you wish your body to be of service to mankind in death, and that, being a Bahá'í, you request that your remains not be cremated and not be taken more than an hour's journey from the place you die. The spirit has no more connection with the body after it departs, but, as the body was once the temple of the spirit, we Bahá'ís are taught that it must be treated with respect." (*Directives from The Guardian*, pp. 46–47)

Remember you need to ensure it is clearly stated in the documentation when your body is no longer required it is to be buried according to Bahá'í burial protocols and not to be cremated.

CHAPTER TWO

- Prayer
- Meditation
- Healing

Can I make up my own prayers?

We are very fortunate that so many prayers for all occasions have been revealed by the Báb, Bahá'u'lláh, and 'Abdu'l-Bahá. You can, however, make up your own prayers. Remember though, that the Creative Word, has special powers. The following quote by Bahá'u'lláh highlights just how powerful the Creative Word is:

> "Every word that proceedeth out of the mouth of God is **endowed** with such potency as can instill new life into every human frame, if ye be of them that comprehend this truth." (*Gleaning from the Writings of Baha'u'llah*, p. 141)

Shoghi Effendi, explains, "Of course, prayer can be purely spontaneous, but many of the sentences and thoughts combined in Bahá'í writings of a devotional nature are easy to grasp, and the revealed Word is endowed with a power of its own." (*Directives from the Guardian*, pp. 58–59)

It is important to keep in mind that prayers can also be expressed through action. 'Abdu'l-Bahá explains:

> "Prayer need not be in words, but rather in thought and attitude. But if this love and this desire are lacking, it is useless to try and force them. Words without love mean nothing. If a person talks to you as an unpleasant duty, with no love or pleasure in his meeting with you, do you wish to converse with him?" (*Compilation,* Vol. 2, p. 236)

Does prayer really assist a person who has mental health issues?

Mental health illness is a term used for a group of illnesses that affect the mind or brain. No one knows the exact cause of mental illness. It is not some weakness or a character flaw in a person. Mental illness is an illness like any other, therefore, medical and specialist treatment should be sought.

Shoghi Effendi emphasises the importance of seeking medical assistance and tells us:

> "There are a great many as you know mental diseases and troubles at present, and the one thing Bahá'ís must not do is take a defeatist attitude toward them. The power in the Faith is such that it can sustain us on a much higher level in spite of whatever our ailments might be than other people who are denied it. This however does not mean that we should ignore medical opinion and treatment. On the contrary, we should do our best to procure the opinion of specialists and competent doctors." (*Lights of Guidance*, p. 284)

'Abdu'l-Bahá tells us how turning to God through prayer will assist us in the following quotes:

> "When thou wishest to treat nervous pain turn thy whole being to the realm on high with thine heart detached from aught else beside Him and thy soul enraptured by the love of God. Then seek confirmation of the Holy Spirit from the Abhá Kingdom, while touching the affected part with utmost love, tenderness and attraction to God. When all these things are combined, be assured that healing will take place." (*Compilation,* Vol. 1, p. 462)

> "Disease is of two kinds: material and spiritual. Take for instance, a cut hand; if you pray for the cut to be healed and

do not stop it bleeding, you will not do much good; a material remedy is needed.

Sometimes if the nervous system is paralysed through fear, a spiritual remedy is necessary. Madness, incurable otherwise, can be cured through prayer. It often happens that sorrow makes one ill, this can be cured by spiritual means." (*Lights of Guidance*, pp. 281–282)

Why is the term 'man' used in the Bahá'í Writings?

Throughout the Bahá'í Writings the term 'man' is used to refer to all people. You must remember during the time of Bahá'u'lláh, 'Abdu'l-Bahá, and Shoghi Effendi this was the norm. The Universal House of Justice explains the generic use of man in the Holy Writings in the following quotes:

> "In many languages the use of the masculine gender, unless intended specifically to denote masculinity, is generic. For instance, in English we speak of the race of man, or mankind, in both instances meaning every member of the human race — men, women and children. There would be no reason to interpret 'O Son of Being', or 'O Son of Man' as addressed only to males. It is the same with pronouns." (Written on behalf of the Universal House of Justice to an Individual Believer, 5 April 1981.)

> "While we recognise that the problem of gender in language presents difficulties at the present time, we must also recognise that the problem varies considerably from language to language, depending on the number of grammatical genders that each language uses.
>
> There are, as you indicate, many conventions of expression in use at the present time which reflect the male dominance of human society in the past. We must hope that as the consciousness of human beings changes and as the equality of the sexes comes to be accepted in theory and in practice throughout the world, the meanings attached to certain words will change accordingly, as will the usage of words. Language is a living thing and changes as the culture which it reflects changes ... The important point here is that one will not persuade people to change their usage of language until one has convinced them of the true understanding of

the reality of things; but when they once understand the truth, the meaning that they attach to words changes, and thus a change in usage becomes much less important, if not irrelevant." (Written on behalf of the Universal House of Justice to an Individual Believer, 8 March 1990.)

Why is meditation important?

There are many forms of meditative practices, all of which contribute in varying degrees to reducing your fear, anxiety, and stress levels. It's about quietening your mind and trying to create a space for silence within, to enable you to reflect and hear your inner voice. 'Abdu'l-Bahá explains meditation is conversing with your soul:

> "It is an **axiomatic** fact that while you meditate you are speaking with your own spirit. In that state of mind you put certain questions to your spirit and the spirit answers: the light breaks forth and the reality is revealed. You cannot apply the name 'man' to any being void of this faculty of meditation; without it he would be a mere animal, lower than the beasts." (*Paris Talks*, pp.174–76)

Describing the benefits of meditation 'Abdu'l-Bahá tells us:

> "This faculty brings forth from the invisible plane the sciences and arts. Through the meditative faculty inventions are made possible, colossal undertakings are carried out; through it governments can run smoothly. Through this faculty man enters into the very Kingdom of God.
>
> Nevertheless some thoughts are useless to man; they are like waves moving in the sea without result. But if the faculty of meditation is bathed in the inner light and characterised with divine attributes, the results will be confirmed." (*Paris Talks*, pp. 174–176).

In addition to telling us about the benefits of meditation, Shoghi Effendi states there are no superior or correct methods of meditating in the following quotes:

> "Through meditation the doors of deeper knowledge and inspiration may be opened. Naturally, if one meditates as a Bahá'í he is connected with the Source; if a man believing in

God meditates he is tuning in to the power and mercy of God; ..." (*Lights of Guidance*, p. 456)

"... There are no set forms of meditation prescribed in the teachings, no plan, as such, for inner development. The friends are urged — nay enjoined — to pray, and they also should meditate, but the manner of doing the latter is left entirely to the individual ..." (*Lights of Guidance*, pp. 445–456)

"The inspiration received through meditation is of a nature that one cannot measure or determine. God can inspire into our minds things that we had no previous knowledge of, if He desires to do so." (*Lights of Guidance*, p. 456)

What other forms of healing are mentioned in the Bahá'í Writings?

There are many forms of healing used throughout history dating back to ancient times. Indigenous people for thousands of years used the roots, leaves and bark from many species of plants to cure several ailments. 'Abdu'l-Bahá tells us how in the future many illnesses will be cured simply by the food we eat.

> "It is, therefore, evident that it is possible to cure by foods, **aliments** and fruits; but as today the science of medicine is imperfect, this fact is not yet fully grasped. When the science of medicine reaches perfection, treatment will be given by foods, ailments, fragrant fruits and vegetables, and by various waters, hot and cold in temperature." (*Some Answered Questions*, pp. 258–259)

Another important form of healing essential to physical healing is spiritual healing. Shoghi Effendi discusses its importance and states:

> "With reference to your question concerning spiritual healing. Its importance, as you surely know, has been greatly emphasised by Abdu'l-Bahá Who considered it, indeed, as an essential part of physical processes of healing. Physical healing cannot be complete and lasting unless it is reinforced by spiritual healing. And this last one can be best obtained through obedience to the laws and commandments of God as revealed to us through His Manifestations. Individual believers, however, can also help by imparting healing to others. But the success of their efforts depends entirely on their strict adherence to the Teachings, and also on the manner in which they impart them to others. According to Bahá'u'lláh man cannot obtain full guidance directly from God. He must rather seek it through His Prophets. Provided this principle is clearly understood and explained, the Guardian sees no harm

that the friends should try to effect spiritual healing on others. Any such cure effected, however, should be done in the name of Bahá'u'lláh and in accordance with His teachings. For God, and God alone, is the Supreme and Almighty Physician and all else are but instruments in His hands." (*Lights of Guidance*, pp. 276–277)

Are Bahá'ís encouraged to get vaccinated for COVID during the pandemic or will they be protected by God?

Coronavirus disease (COVID-19) is a virus which is part of the family of viruses called Coronaviride. Since it is a virus antibiotics do not work. At the time of writing this book, there is no licensed medication to cure COVID-19. Unfortunately, there has been a great deal of misinformation and myths around the causes and treatment of COVID-19. There have been several variants to date, and this will no doubt continue. If you have symptoms, call your health care provider.

There are currently a handful of vaccinations available to assist in reducing the severity of symptoms and the likelihood of hospitalisation. In the Bahá'í Writings nothing has been written about vaccination. Nevertheless, the Universal House of Justice wrote the following in response to an individual believer who enquired as to whether they should get vaccinated:

> "In relation to the coronavirus pandemic, (Bahá'ís) should follow the counsel of medical and other scientific experts on the advisability and **efficacy** of the various vaccination options that are becoming available and the wisdom of particular public health measures. They should not be concerned merely with their own personal choices and well-being, but in reaching their decisions, they should also consider their social responsibilities and the common good.
>
> This means, for Bahá'ís and all other people who believe in the oneness of humanity, that vaccination is not just a personal decision, but instead represents a public health decision for the collective protection and well-being of the entire human family." (Department of Secretariat, Universal House of Justice, Letter to an Individual Believer, 10 July 2020.)

Bahá'í's are not able to claim an exemption based on their religious beliefs. The Universal House of Justice reiterates a fundamental Bahá'í principle — loyalty and obedience to government and states:

"As Shoghi Effendi explained in a letter dated 21 December 1948 written on his behalf to an individual believer, 'We must obey in all cases except where a spiritual principle is involved, such as denying our Faith.' If a Bahá'í is faced with a government mandate of vaccination, the Bahá'í writings would not provide him or her justification for refusing to comply with such a legal requirement; therefore, a religious exemption could not be claimed. Of course, if the law itself provided another applicable exemption, a believer would be free to decide, including for family members for whom he or she is responsible, whether to invoke such an exemption." (Department of Secretariat, Universal House of Justice, Letter to an Individual Believer, 10 July 2020.)

CHAPTER THREE

Additional Christian related topics

Can Bahá'ís celebrate Christmas?

Christmas is a Christian festival celebrating the birth of Jesus. Although, Christmas is celebrated on the 25th of December, *The New Testament* provides no clues as to Jesus' actual birthdate. Since the early 20th century, Christmas has also been a secular family holiday, celebrated by Christians and non-Christians alike.

Bahá'ís can celebrate Christmas, however, there are a few things to keep in mind while doing so as highlighted by the Universal House of Justice. Below are extracts from a letter written by the Universal House of Justice to an 11-year-old girl who asked the very same question.

> "As Bahá'ís believe that all religions come from God, they could, in principle, celebrate Christmas and the other holidays of the Christian faith and other religions. But would it be a good idea? We should consider two things:
>
> First of all, Bahá'u'lláh, the Messenger of God for our age, brought us new teachings for a new Age. He gave us a new calendar with new Holy days. Good occasions for us to celebrate and give gifts are, for example, Intercalary Days and Naw-Ruz.
>
> Another thing to remember is this: if Bahá'ís would start to celebrate Christmas, other people who do not know that they are Bahá'ís could think that they were Christians. People would be even more confused if Bahá'ís would also start celebrating the Holy days of other religions. In order to avoid such confusion, the beloved Guardian counselled the friends to no longer celebrate days like Christmas and the New Year with other Bahá'ís.
>
> But, as you know, not everybody is Bahá'í: many Bahá'ís come from Christian families who celebrate Christmas! There is nothing wrong for Bahá'ís to celebrate Christmas with their families. Sometimes, Bahá'ís are invited to Christmas celebrations with their friends: all this is fine,

because Bahá'u'lláh taught that Bahá'ís must maintain cordial relationships with the followers of all religions. You must remember, though, that Bahá'í families and Bahá'í communities do not celebrate Christmas with each other." (The Universal House of Justice, Letter to an 11-year-old girl, 18 April 1988.)

Can Bahá'ís confess their sins, and then be forgiven?

Confession of your sins is an act that even if you have not grown up in a Catholic family or attended a Catholic school you would be familiar with, as it is often quoted in movies, and in television series. Bahá'u'lláh makes it very clear that Baha'is are not to confess their sins and provides an explanation as to why this act is forbidden.

> "Confession before the servants (i.e., before men) is not permissible, for it is not the means or the cause of Divine Forgiveness. Such confession before the creatures leads to one's humiliation and **abasement**, and God exalted by His Glory does not wish for the humiliation of His servants. Verily He is Compassionate and Beneficent. The sinner must, between himself and God, beg for mercy from the Sea of Mercy and implore pardon from the Heaven of Forgiveness."
> (*Glad Tidings Tablets of Bahá'u'lláh*, p. 24)

The Guardian reiterates Bahá'u'lláh's command, and explains under what circumstances an individual can seek another person's forgiveness in the following quote:

> "We are forbidden to confess to any person, as do the Catholics to their priests, our sins and shortcomings, or to do so in public, as some religious sects do. However, if we spontaneously desire to acknowledge we have been wrong in something, or that we have some fault of character, and ask another person's forgiveness or pardon, we are quite free to do so. The Guardian wants to point out, however, that we are not obliged to do so. It rests entirely with the individual."
> (*Lights of Guidance*, p. 178)

Why doesn't the Bahá'í Faith have any priests, or clergy to guide its followers?

In the Bahá'í Faith there are no priests, nor clergy as Bahá'ís are encouraged, invited, and responsible for teaching and sharing the message of Bahá'u'lláh, the Manifestation of God for today. This is explained by Shoghi Effendi in the quote below:

> "Bahá'u'lláh has enjoined upon the Bahá'ís the sacred obligation of teaching. We have no priests, therefore the service once rendered by priests to their religions is the service every single Bahá'í is expected to render individually to his religion. He must be the one who enlightens new souls, confirms them, heals the wounded and the weary upon the road of life, gives them to quaff from the chalice of everlasting life — the knowledge of the Manifestation of God in His Day." (*Lights of Guidance*, p. 247)

Unfortunately, throughout history many conflicts and even wars have been carried out in the name of religion. The following quotes highlights this fact:

> "If priests of religion really adored the God of love and served the Divine Light, they would teach their people to keep the chief Commandment, 'To be in love and charity with all men'. But we find the contrary, for it is often the priests who encourage nations to fight. Religious hatred is ever the most cruel!
>
> All religions teach that we should love one another; that we should seek out our own shortcomings before we presume to condemn the faults of others, that we must not consider ourselves superior to our neighbours! We must be careful not to exalt ourselves lest we be humiliated.
>
> Who are we that we should judge? How shall we know who, in the sight of God, is the most upright man? God's thoughts are not, like our thoughts! How many men who

have seemed saint-like to their friends have fallen into the greatest humiliation. Think of Judas Iscariot; he began well but remember his end! On the other hand, Paul, the Apostle, was in his early life an enemy of Christ, whilst later he became His most faithful servant. How then can we flatter ourselves and despise others?" ('Abdu'l-Bahá, *Paris Talks*, p.121)

"It seems both strange and pitiful that the Church and clergy should always, in every age, be the most bitter opponents of the very Truth they are continually **admonishing** their followers to be prepared to receive! They have become so violently attached to the form that the substance itself eludes them!" (Shoghi Effendi, *Lights of Guidance*, p. 419)

How is Bahá'u'lláh, the Return of Christ?

The Baha'i Writings make it clear, Bahá'u'lláh is the "return of Christ" and has fulfilled all His promises predicted in the Gospel. Abdu'l-Bahá explains what the term "return" means in the Scriptures and states:

"In the Divine Scriptures and Holy Books 'return' is spoken of, but the ignorant have not understood the meaning, and those who believed in reincarnation have made conjectures on the subject. For what the divine Prophets meant by 'return' is not the return of the essences, but that of the qualities; it is not the return of the Manifestation, but that of the perfections …

A lamp shone in the room last night, and when tonight another lamp shines, we say the light of last night is again shining. Water flows from a fountain; then it ceases; and when it begins to flow a second time, we say this water is the same water flowing again; or we say this light is identical with the former light. It is the same with the spring of last year, when blossoms, flowers and sweet-scented herbs bloomed, and delicious fruits were brought forth, next year we say that those delicious fruits have come back, and those blossoms, flowers and blooms have returned and come again. This does not mean that exactly the same particles composing the flowers of last year have, after decomposition, been again combined and have then come back and returned. On the contrary, the meaning is that the delicacy, freshness, delicious perfume and wonderful colour of the flowers of last year are visible and apparent in exactly the same manner in the flowers of last year. Briefly, this expression refers only to the resemblance and likeness which exist between the former and latter flowers. The 'return' which is mentioned in the Divine Scriptures is this …" (*Some Answered Questions*, pp. 288–289)

Shoghi Effendi invites people to read Bahá'u'lláh's explanation of 'the return of Christ' to clarify its true meaning, and states:

"Now regarding the signs that would herald the advent of the new Manifestation: the Guardian wishes you to read over very carefully Bahá'u'lláh's explanation as recorded in the Íqán. There it is made clear that what is meant by the appearance of the Son of God after the calamitous events preceding His coming is the revelation of His full glory and its recognition and acceptance by the peoples of the world, and not His physical appearance. For Bahá'u'lláh, already appeared, and the signs predicted in the Gospel have not yet fully been realised. Their complete fulfilment, however, would mark the beginning of the recognition of His full station by the peoples of the world. Then and only then will His appearance be made completely manifest." (*Lights of Guidance*, p. 492)

What is the true meaning of the miracles performed by Christ?

The term miracle comes from the Greek thaumasion and the Latin miraculum. It is defined as an event or occurrence that is extraordinary, amazing, or inexplicable by normal standards. In virtually all religions a belief in miraculous happenings can be found. 'Abdu'l-Bahá explains why Manifestations of God can perform miracles and states:

> "The Manifestations of God are sources of miraculous deeds and marvellous signs. Any difficult or impossible matter is to Them possible and permitted. For They show forth extraordinary feats through an extraordinary power, and They influence the world of nature through a power that transcends nature. From each one of Them, marvellous things have appeared." (*Some Answered Questions*, p. 113)

Discussing certain miracles attributed to Christ mentioned in the Bible, 'Abdu'l-Bahá explains:

> "Consider that Christ reckoned as dead those who were nonetheless outwardly and physically alive; for true life is life eternal and true existence is spiritual existence. Thus if the Sacred Scriptures speak of raising the dead, the meaning is that they attained everlasting life; if they say that one who was blind was made to see, the meaning is of this seeing is true insight; if they say that one who was deaf was made to hear, the meaning is that he acquired an inner ear and attained spiritual hearing. This is established by the very text of the Gospel where Christ says that they are like those of whom Isaiah once said, They have eyes and see not, they have ears and hear not; and I heal them." (*Some Answered Questions,* p. 115)

Can a person be a Bahá'í and a Christian at the same time?

When a Christian declares their faith in Bahá'u'lláh, they still believe in Jesus, however, they are encouraged to withdraw their church membership. There are several reasons outlined by Shoghi Effendi as to why this is encouraged in the following quotes:

> "When a person becomes a Bahá'í, he gives up the past only in the sense that he is part of this new living Faith of God, and must seek to pattern himself, in act and thought, along the lines laid down by Bahá'u'lláh. The fact that he is by origin a Jew or a Christian, a black man or a white man, is not important anymore, but, as you say, lends colour and charm to the Bahá'í community in that it demonstrates unity in diversity." (*Directives from the Guardian*, p. 9)

> "To continue to be a member of the church places a Bahá'í in an insincere position — for we believe the Christ has come again, in Bahá'u'lláh, and that all His promises have been gloriously fulfilled. No church would tolerate one of the members believing such a thing, for the church is still blindly waiting the second coming. Therefore it is obvious why the Bahá'ís must leave the church, they are not leaving Christ, but rather rallying to His support in the new day of His coming." (*Light of Divine Guidance*, p. 90)

> "The friends should by all means be encouraged to withdraw from church membership and be made to realise that, though we as Bahá'ís are ardent believers in Christ, we do not and cannot support, church institutions and **doctrines**, when Christ has come again and brought new laws for the world today and its present needs; to adhere to forms, most man-made, and now out-moded and no longer needed, is meaningless. This does not mean they should no longer

associate with the church members; they should cease to be registered members of it." (*Light of Divine Guidance*, p. 160)

CHAPTER FOUR

- Sexuality
- Freedom and Rights

Are Bahá'ís allowed to have an abortion?

An abortion also known as a termination is when medicine or a surgical procedure is used to end a pregnancy. There are many reasons why women choose to have an abortion. It is a very difficult decision to make. It is permissible for a Bahá'í woman to have an abortion under certain circumstances. Below are extracts from a couple of letters written by the Universal House of Justice to individual believers stating certain circumstances when an abortion would be permissible:

> "Abortion and surgical operations for the purpose of preventing the birth of unwanted children are forbidden in the Cause unless there are circumstances which justify such actions on medical grounds, in which case the decision, at present, is left to the consciences of those concerned who must carefully weigh the medical advice in the light of the general guidance given in the Teachings. Beyond this nothing has been found in the Writings concerning specific methods or procedures to be used in family planning. It should be pointed out, however, that the Teachings state that the soul appears at conception, and that therefore it would be improper to use such a method, the effect of which would be to produce an abortion after conception has taken place." (Universal House of Justice, Letter to an Individual Believer, 23 May 1975.)

> "One of the most heinous of sexual offences is the crime of rape. When a believer is a victim, she is entitled to the loving aid and support of the members of her community, and she is free to initiate action against the perpetrator under the law of the land should she wish to do so. If she becomes pregnant as a consequence of this assault, no pressure should be brought upon her by the Bahá'í institutions to marry. As to whether she should continue or terminate the pregnancy, it is for her to decide on course of action she should follow,

taking into consideration medical and other relevant factors, and in the light of the Bahá'í Teachings." (Universal House of Justice, Letter to an Individual Believer, 24 January 1993.)

Why is Chastity Important?

There are several quotes about the importance of chastity in the Bahá'í writings. Shoghi Effendi defined what is meant by chastity in the following quotes:

> "Chastity in the strict sense means not to have sexual intercourse, or sexual intimacies, before marriage. In the general sense it means not to be licentious. This does not mean we Bahá'ís believe sexual relations to be impure or wrong. On the contrary they are natural and should be considered one of God's many blessings ... when the world becomes more spiritual there will not be such an exaggerated emphasis on sex, as there is today, and consequently it will be easier for young people to be chaste and control their passions." (*Light of Guidance*, Vol. 2, p. 71.)

> "What Bahá'u'lláh means by chastity certainly does not include the kissing that goes on in modern society. It is detrimental to the morals of young people, and often leads them to go too far, or arouses appetites which they cannot perhaps at the time satisfy legitimately through marriage, and the suppression of which is a strain on them.
>
> The Bahá'í standard is very high, more particularly when compared with the thoroughly rotten morals of the present world. But this standard of ours will produce healthier, happier, nobler people, and induce stabler marriages." (From a letter written on behalf of the Guardian to an Individual Believer, 19 October 1947.)

The Universal House of Justice acknowledges the difficulty of practicing chastity for young people during this present time and states:

> "As to chastity, this is one of the most challenging concepts to get across in this very **permissive** age, but Bahá'ís must make the utmost effort to uphold Bahá'í standards, no matter

how difficult they may seem at first. Such efforts will be made easier if the youth will understand that the laws and standards of the Faith are meant to free them from untold spiritual and moral difficulties in the same way that a proper appreciation of the laws of nature enables one to live in harmony with the forces of the planet ..." (From a letter written on behalf of the Universal House of Justice to an Individual Believer, 14 January 1985.)

Tahirih Lemon

What does the Bahá'í Writings say about masturbation?

Masturbation has been a taboo topic throughout history, and according to some religious beliefs a sin. There are no explicit references to masturbation in the Bahá'í Writings. Several extracts have been provided below from a letter written by The Universal House of Justice to an individual believer regarding some principles and teachings in the Holy Writings that can guide a Bahá'í's attitude regarding masturbation.

> "The Bahá'í Faith recognises the value of the sex impulse, but condemns its illegitimate and improper expressions such as free love, companionate marriage and others, all of which it considers positively harmful to man and to the society in which he lives. The proper use of the sex instinct is the natural right of every individual, and it is precisely for this very purpose that the institution of marriage has been established. The Bahá'ís do not believe in the suppression of the sex impulse but in its regulation and control.
>
> In another letter on the Guardian's behalf, also to an individual believer, the secretary writes: 'Amongst the many other evils afflicting society in this spiritual low water mark in history is the question of immorality, and over-emphasis of sex ...'
>
> This indicates how the whole matter of sex and the problems related to it have assumed far too great an importance in the thinking of present-day society.
>
> Masturbation is clearly not a proper use of the sex instinct, as this is understood in the Faith. Moreover it involves, as you have pointed out, mental fantasies, while Bahá'u'lláh, in the *Kitáb-i-Aqdas*, has exhorted us not to indulge our passions and in one of His well-known Tablets Abdu'l-Bahá encourages us to keep our 'secret thoughts pure'.

Of course, many wayward thoughts come involuntarily to the mind and these are merely a result of weakness and are not blameworthy unless they become fixed or even worse, are expressed in improper acts." (From a letter of the Universal House of Justice to an Individual Believer, 8 March 1981.)

What about Bahá'í's individual rights and freedoms within the Bahá'í community?

Freedom is defined as the power or right to act, speak, or think as you like. However, what if by doing this you hurt other people in the process? With freedom comes rights and responsibilities. When we accept Bahá'u'lláh as the Manifestation of God for today, we also simultaneously agree to follow His teachings and laws. The extract below is from a letter written by the Universal House of Justice regarding the challenges some Baha'is may have in applying the Bahá'í principles and laws in their daily lives:

> "We have noticed with concern evidences of a confusion of attitudes among some of the friends when they encounter difficulties in applying Bahá'í principles to questions of the day. On the one hand, they acknowledge their belief in Bahá'u'lláh and His teachings; on the other, they invoke Western liberal democratic practices when actions of Bahá'í institutions or of some of their fellow Bahá'ís do not accord with their expectations. At the heart of this confusion are misconceptions of such fundamental issues as individual rights and freedom of expression in the Bahá'í community. The source of the potential difficulties of the situation appears to us to be an inadequacy of Bahá'í perspective on the part of both individual believers and their institutions."
> (*The Promulgation of Universal Peace*, pp. 102–103)

True freedom requires the exercise of moderation in all things, as demonstrated in the following extracts from a letter written by the Universal House:

> "In his summary of significant Bahá'í teachings, Shoghi Effendi wrote that Bahá'u'lláh "inculcates the principle of 'moderation in all things; declares that whatsoever, be it 'liberty, civilisation and the like,' 'passeth beyond the limits of moderation' must 'exercise a pernicious influence upon men'; observes that

western civilisation has gravely perturbed and alarmed the peoples of the world; and predicts that the day is approaching when the 'flame' of civilisation 'carried to excess' 'will devour the cities'." (Letter to an Individual Believer, 29 December 1988.)

"Expounding the theme of liberty, Bahá'u'lláh asserted that 'the **embodiment** of liberty and its symbol is the animal'; that 'liberty causeth man to overstep the bounds of propriety, and to infringe on the dignity of his station', that 'true liberty consisteth in man's submission unto My commandments.' 'We approve liberty in certain circumstances,' He declared, 'and refuse to sanction it in others.' But He gave the assurance that, "Were men to observe that which We have sent down unto them from the Heaven of Revelation, they would, of a certainty, attain unto perfect liberty." And again, He said, 'Mankind in its entirety must firmly adhere to whatsoever hath been revealed and vouchsafed unto it. Then and only then will it attain unto true liberty'." (Universal House of Justice, To an Individual Believer, 29 December 1988.)

CHAPTER FIVE

- Social issues
- Role of young people

Can Bahá'ís end their life through euthanasia?

The term euthanasia comes from the Greek word *euthanatos*, which means 'easy death'. Euthanasia is when medical intervention is used following a patient's request to end their life. Patients are required to be 18 years or older, and have a disease, illness or medical condition that is advanced, incurable and will cause death in 6–12 months, and they are suffering from pain that cannot be relieved to the extent the patient finds bearable.

There are no references to euthanasia in the Bahá'í Writings and for the present time the Universal House of Justice has not legislated on the matter. Below are extracts from letters written by the Universal House of Justice to individuals, responding to their questions regarding euthanasia:

> "We have received your letter of March 18, 1974, in which you ask for the Bahá'í viewpoint on euthanasia and on the removal of life support in medical cases where physiological interventions prolong life in disabling illnesses. In general our teachings indicate that God, the Giver of life, can alone dispose of it as He deems best, and we have found nothing in the Sacred Text on these matters specifically but in a letter to an individual written on behalf of the beloved Guardian by his secretary regarding mercy killings, or legalised euthanasia, it is stated:
>
>> '... this is also a matter which the Universal House of Justice will have to legislate.'
>
> Until such time as the Universal House of Justice considers legislation on euthanasia, decisions in the matters to which you refer must be left to the consciences of those responsible." (Letter to the National Spiritual Assembly of Alaska, 17 May 1974.)

What does the Bahá'í Writings say about climate change?

There is no place on this planet that is not being impacted by climate change. What is climate change? According to the United Nations:

> "Climate change can be a natural process where temperature, rainfall, wind and other elements vary over decades or more. In millions of years, our world has been warmer and colder than it is now. But today we are experiencing unprecedented rapid warming from human activities, primarily due to burning fossil fuels that generate greenhouse gas emissions."

The Universal House of Justice addressed the issue of climate change in a letter to some concerned individual believers. Several paragraphs have been selected from this letter:

> "One of the most pressing problems of humanity in the current century is how a growing, rapidly developing, and not yet united global population can, in a just manner, live in harmony with the planet and its finite resources. Certain biological realities present themselves when an organism negatively affects or exceeds the capacity of its ecosystem. The limited availability and inequitable distribution of resources profoundly impact social relations within and between nations in many ways, even to the point of precipitating upheaval and war. And particular arrangements of human affairs can have devastating consequences for the environment. The question of the impact of climate change, and to what extent it is man-made and its effects can be **ameliorated**, is today a major aspect of this larger problem. The Revelation of Bahá'u'lláh directly and indirectly touches on a range of such concerns in a manner that speaks to a harmony between a society and the natural world. It is essential, therefore, that Bahá'ís contribute thought and action regarding such matters.

Among the Bahá'í teachings are those concerning the importance of science. 'Great indeed is the claim of scientists … on the peoples of the world,' Bahá'u'lláh observed. 'Abdu'l-Bahá wrote that the 'sciences of today are bridges to reality' and repeatedly emphasised that 'religion must be in conformity with science and reason.'

More than a century ago, 'Abdu'l-Bahá referred to 'unity of thought in world undertakings, the consummation of which will erelong be witnessed.' The recently adopted international agreement on climate change, irrespective of any shortcomings and limitations it may have, offers another noteworthy demonstration of that development anticipated by 'Abdu'l-Bahá. The agreement represents a starting point for constructive thought and action that can be refined or revised on the basis of experience and new findings over time." (Letters to Three Individuals, 29 November 2017.)

When there is no more poverty will everyone have lots of money in the future?

One of the principles of the Bahá'í Faith is the elimination of the extremes of poverty and wealth. This does not mean when poverty is eradicated everyone will become wealthy. This is not possible nor is it desirable for everyone to be paid equally, as 'Abdu'l-Bahá explains, "... the whole order of the world would be destroyed". (*Paris Talks*, pp. 151–152)

Shoghi Effendi further elaborates on this issue and states:

> "... The Master has definitely stated that wages should be unequal, simply because men are unequal in their ability, and hence should receive wages that would correspond to their varying capacities and resources. This view seems to contradict the opinion of some modern economists. But the friends should have full confidence in the words of the Master, and should give preference to His statements over those voiced by our so-called modern thinkers." (*Lights of Guidance*, p. 550)

Discussing further why it is not feasible for everyone to be paid equally since people have different abilities and capacities, Shoghi Effendi states:

> "The intent is not, however; to say that all the poor will become rich and they will become equal. Such a concept is like saying that all the ignorant and the illiterate will become the sages of the age and the learned of the learned. Rather, when education becomes compulsory and universal, ignorance and illiteracy will decrease and there will remain no one deprived of education. But at the basis for distinction is in the person's capacity and ability, and differences are related to the degree of his intelligence and mental powers, therefore, all the people will not be equal in their knowledge, learning and understanding. The intent is to say that the world of creation

calls for distinctions in people's stations, and degrees in the differences existing among them, so that the affairs of the world may become organised and ordered. Diversity in all created things, whether in kind, in physical appearance, or in station, is the means for their protection, their permanence, unity and harmony. Each part **complements** the other." (*Economics, Agriculture and Related Subjects*, p. 22)

Should Bahá'í parents use physical discipline to teach their children right from wrong?

The word discipline originates from the Latin word *discipulus*, the word used for pupil. Discipline means to teach. Physical or corporal discipline is a form of punishment and includes but is not limited to slapping, pushing, shoving, smacking, spanking, or hitting. There is a growing amount of evidence showing not only is physical discipline harmful and ineffective, but it can also have lasting harm for children. This is affirmed by 'Abdu'l-Bahá's guidance regarding how parents should discipline their children in the following quote:

> "Let the mothers consider that whatever concerneth the education of children is of the first importance. Let them put forth every effort in this regard, for when the bough is green and tender it will grow in whatever way ye train it. Therefore is it **incumbent** upon the mothers to rear their little ones even as a gardener tendeth his young plants. Let them strive by day and by night to establish within their children faith and certitude, the fear of God, the love of the Beloved of the worlds, and all good qualities and traits. Whensoever a mother seeth that her child hath done well, let her praise and applaud him and cheer his heart; and if the slightest undesirable trait should manifest itself, let her counsel the child and punish him, and use means based on reason, even a slight verbal chastisement should this be necessary. It is not, however, permissible to strike a child, or vilify him, for the child's character will be totally perverted if he be subjected to blows or verbal abuse." (*Selections from the Writings of Abdu'l-Bahá*, pp. 124–125)

More and more countries are legislating against the use of physical discipline of children. Educational efforts are being made to inform parents of the harmful effects of traditional, outdated modes of physical discipline and are emphasising positive approaches such as role-modeling, explanations, praise, removal of privileges, and natural consequences.

Can Bahá'ís participate in protests and rallies?

Protests and rallies are a form of activism where groups of people gather in a public space to protest about a current issue of concern or an injustice, in the hope to bring about change. Bahá'ís can participate in non-violent protests and rallies that align with the Bahá'í teachings for example on issues such as peace, equality of the sexes, racism, and the environment.

Shoghi Effendi explains when it is alright for Bahá'ís to participate in protests, and states:

> "Movements for social progress and social justice, as long as they are disassociated from both political and religious **partisanship**, should be supported by those Bahá'ís who feel urged to undertake such work." (*Lights of Guidance*, p. 532)

The importance of transforming peoples' hearts and their recognition of their divine origin and Bahá'u'lláh as the latest Manifestation of God, is key to bringing about change in society. This is highlighted in the following extracts written on behalf of the Guardian and the Universal House of Justice:

> "There are so many movements in the world at present akin to various Bahá'í principles; indeed we can almost say that the principles of Bahá'u'lláh have been adapted by thinking people all over this planet. But what they do not realise, and what the Bahá'ís must therefore teach them, is that these principles, however perfect, will never be able to create a new society unless and until they are animated by the spirit which alone changes the hearts and characters of men, and that spirit is recognition of their divine origin in a teacher sent from God, in other words, Bahá'u'lláh. When they recognise this, their hearts will change and a change of heart is what people need, not merely a change of intellectual outlook." (*Lights of Guidance*, p. 425)

Tahirih Lemon

"As your letter points out, there are instances where the Guardian endorsed Bahá'ís identifying themselves with protest activities on vital issues which the Bahá'í teachings illuminate. It must be remembered that there is an important distinction between protest against attitudes and practices prevalent in some quarters of society and protest antagonistic to the government. The Bahá'í Faith directs its attention principally to the promotion of attitudinal change consequent to acceptance of the claim of Bahá'u'lláh, confident that the transformation of attitudes and values will, in due course, yield its fruit in measures which will resolve the problems with which humanity is now burdened." (Written on behalf of the Universal House of Justice, to a Group of Bahá'ís, 24 October 1990.)

What is the role of young people in the Bahá'í Faith?

Youth with their exuberance are needed to play an active role with in the Bahá'í Faith. They must become the change required through a lifetime of service and dedication. Shoghi Effendi highlights the important role youth play in the future growth of the Bahá'í Faith, and states:

"The future of this Cause, which is so dear to us all, depends upon the energy and devotion of the rising generation. It is you who before long will be called to shoulder its responsibilities and undertake its spread. To do that, however, you ought to be well equipped. You ought to have your intellectual as well as spiritual side equally developed ..." (*The Compilation of Compilations,* Vol. 2, p. 418)

The Universal House of Justice encouraging youth, states the following:

"To every generation of young believers comes an opportunity to make a contribution to the fortunes of humanity, unique to their time of life. For the present generation, the moment has come to reflect, to commit, to steel themselves for a life of service from which blessing will flow in abundance." (*The Five Year Plan 2011–2016*, pp. 93–94)

'Abdu'l-Bahá wrote to the youth stating:

"The period of youth is characterised by strength and vigour and stands out as the choicest time in human life. Therefore you should strive day and night so that endowed with heavenly strength, inspired with brilliant motives and aided by His celestial power and heavenly grace and confirmation, you may become the ornaments of the world of humanity, and **preeminent** among those who are initiated into true learning and the love of God. You must be distinguished amidst men by your sanctity and detachment, loftiness of purpose, magnanimity, determination, noble-mindedness, tenacity, the elevation of your aims and your spiritual qualities; that you may become the means of exaltation and glory for the Cause of God and the dawning-places of His heavenly bestowals; that you may conduct yourselves in conformity with the counsels and exhortations of the Blessed Beauty — may my life be offered up for His loved ones — and by reflecting Bahá'í qualities and attributes, you may stand out distinguished from others." (*Bahá'í Prayers and Tablets for the Young*, p. 30)

CHAPTER SIX

Personal challenges

How should people view tests and difficulties?

Everyone experiences tests and difficulties throughout their life. Sometimes these seem insurmountable. Generally, whether a person views something as a test or difficulty, comes down to perspective. Is the glass half-empty or half-full? Believe it or not tests and difficulties are for our own benefit. It is during challenging times we have an opportunity to further strengthen our character and grow spiritually. It is reassuring and comforting to know we are never tested beyond our capacity. Several quotes from Shoghi Effendi are listed below highlighting the importance of tests and difficulties for our spiritual development:

> "We must always look ahead and seek to accomplish in the future what we may have failed to do in the past. Failures, tests, and trials, if we use them correctly, can become the means of purifying our spirit, strengthening our characters, and enable us to rise to greater heights of service." (*Lights of Guidance*, p. 601)

> "Suffering is both a reminder and a guide. It stimulates us better to adapt ourselves to our environmental conditions, and thus leads the way to self improvement. In every suffering one can find a meaning and a wisdom. But it is not always easy to find the secret of that wisdom. It is sometimes only when all our suffering has passed that we become aware of its usefulness. What man considers to be evil turns often to be a cause of infinite blessings." (*Unfolding Destiny*, p. 434)

> "Life afflicts us with very severe trials sometimes, but we must always remember that when we accept patiently the Will of God He compensates us in other ways. With faith and love we must be patient, and He will surely reward us." (*Lights of Guidance*, p. 603)

"He urges you to persevere and add up your accomplishments, rather than dwell on the dark side of things. Everyone's life has both a dark and bright side. The Master said: turn your back to the darkness and your face to Me." (*Unfolding Destiny*, p. 457)

Bahá'u'lláh assures us, God will, "... never deal unjustly with anyone, neither will He task a soul beyond its power." (*Gleanings from the Writings of Bahá'u'lláh*, p. 106)

As Bahá'í's we are encouraged to love everyone, even our enemies but what if a person continually bullies and hurts you?

Many of you unfortunately at some stage or another have or will experience or witness, bullying. It can take the form of verbal, physical, social, and increasingly cyberbullying. There are several reasons why a person might bully someone else. Regardless of the reason, it is never ok.

If you are being bullied, tell the bully what they are doing is not ok. If they continue, tell an adult you trust who can help not only you, but the bully who needs assistance to discontinue their intimidating behaviours. It is important to remember not to fight back nor retaliate. Two wrongs do not make a right and will only cause things to escalate. 'Abdu'l-Bahá provides the following guidance when someone mistreats you:

> "... if someone oppresses, injures and wrongs another, and the wronged man retaliates, this is vengeance and is censurable ... No, rather he must return good for evil, and not only forgive, but also, if possible, be of service to his oppressor. This conduct is worthy of man: for what advantage does he gain by vengeance? The two actions are equivalent; if one action is reprehensible, both are reprehensible. The only difference is that one was committed first, the other later." (*Selections from the Writings of 'Abdu'l-Bahá,* p. 158)

It isn't about turning 'a blind eye' to the bullying either. If a bully's behaviours are not addressed, they will continue to bully others. Sometimes the bully might not even be aware that their actions are considered a form of bullying. The bully might be a victim of bullying themselves, simply lashing out and mimicking learned behaviours. The following quote by 'Abdu'l-Bahá explains why it is important to address erroneous behaviours:

"Strive ye then with all your heart to treat compassionately all humankind — except for those who have some selfish, private motive, or some disease of the soul. Kindness cannot be shown the tyrant, the deceiver, or the thief, because, far from awakening them to the error of their ways, it maketh them to continue in their perversity as before. No matter how much kindliness ye may expend upon the liar, he will but lie the more, for he believeth you to be deceived, while ye understand him but too well, and only remain silent out of your extreme compassion." (*Selections from the Writings of 'Abdu'l-Bahá*, p. 158)

Will Bahá'ís suffer along with the rest of the world's population, or will they be protected by God?

The daily news bombards us with myriad reports of natural disasters, catastrophes, disease, injustices, conflict, and wars occurring throughout the world. Although sad and tragic, all these unfortunate events unfolding have been foretold by Bahá'u'lláh. They will continue to escalate until humanity recognises its oneness and applies spiritual principles to the solutions for the world's problems. Shoghi Effendi explains this in the following quote:

> "In the spiritual development of man a stage of **purgation** is indispensable, for it is while passing through it that the over-rate material needs are made to appear in their proper light. Unless society learns to attribute more importance to spiritual matters, it would never be fit to enter the golden era foretold by Bahá'u'lláh. The present calamities are parts of this process of purgation, through them alone will man learn his lesson. They are to teach the nations, that they have to view things internationally, they are to make the individual attribute more importance to his moral, than his material welfare." (*Lights of Guidance,* pp. 133–134)

Bahá'ís like everyone else will suffer along with the rest of the world's population. This suffering should spur us on to continue our efforts in teaching others about Bahá'u'lláh and His teachings. This is demonstrated in the following quotes by Shoghi Effendi who states:

> "In such a process of purgation, when all humanity is in the throes of dire suffering, the Bahá'ís should not hope to remain unaffected. Should we consider the beam that is in our own eye, we would immediately find that these sufferings are also

meant for ourselves, who claim to have attained. Such world crisis is necessary to awaken us to the importance of our duty and the carrying on of our task. Suffering will increase our energy in setting before humanity the road to salvation, it will move us from our repose for we are far from doing our best in teaching the Cause and conveying the Message with which we have been entrusted ..." (*Lights of Guidance*, pp. 33–34)

"The Bahá'ís all over the world are subject sometimes to suffering, along with their fellow-men. Whatever **vicissitudes** befall their country, they will be protected though, and watched over by Bahá'u'lláh, and should not fear the future but rather fear any failure on their part to carry out the work of His Cause." (*Dawn of a New Day*, p. 202)

What does the Bahá'í Writings say about backbiting and gossiping?

Backbiting is a term used to describe the action of saying something unkind, unpleasant, or mean about someone else when they are not present. Gossiping is spreading rumours about someone else's private or personal life that may or may not be true. Both actions are condemned by Bahá'u'lláh, who states the following:

> "O Son of Man! Breathe not the sins of others so long as thou art thyself a sinner. Shouldst thou transgress this command, accursed wouldst thou be, and to this I bear witness." (*The Hidden Words of Bahá'u'lláh*, No.27)

> "O Son of Being! Ascribe not to any soul that which thou wouldst not have ascribed to thee, and say not that which thou doest not. This is My command unto thee, do thou observe it." (*The Hidden Words of Bahá'u'lláh*, No.29)

> "For the tongue is a smouldering fire, and excess of speech a deadly poison. Material fire consumeth the body, whereas the fire of the tongue devoureth both heart and soul. The force of the former lasteth but for a time, whilst the effect of the latter endureth a century." (*Gleanings from the Writings of Bahá'u'lláh*, p. 264)

You may have grown up being told, "If you don't have something nice to say, don't say anything at all." 'Abdu'l-Bahá takes this a step further to a whole new level and states:

> "To be silent concerning the faults of others, to pray for them, through kindness, to correct their faults. To look always at the good and not at the bad. If a man has ten good qualities and one bad one, to look at the ten and forget the one; and if a man has ten bad qualities and one good one, to look at the

one and forget the ten. Never to allow ourselves to speak one unkind word about another, even though that other be our enemy." (*Bahá'u'lláh and The New Era,* p. 286)

CHAPTER SEVEN

The Covenant and Miscellaneous Topics

What is the purpose of religion?

Unfortunately, particularly in western countries where materialism is rampant, more people are turning away from religion. It is understandable that many people have come to view religion as irrelevant in their lives, and in many cases see religion as being more divisive as opposed to unifying. This is due however, to ignorance, and misinformation about the true nature of religion and its purpose. This is explained in the following quotes:

> "Religion is, verily, the chief instrument for the establishment of order in the world, and of tranquility amongst its peoples. The weakening of the pillars of religion hath strengthened the foolish, and emboldened them, and make them more arrogant. Verily I say: The greater the decline of religion, the more grievous the waywardness of the ungodly. This cannot but lead in the end to chaos and confusion." (Bahá'u'lláh, *Epistle to the Son of the Wolf*, p. 28)

> "Religion should unite all hearts and cause wars and disputes to vanish from the face of the earth, give birth to spirituality, and bring life and light to each heart. If religion becomes a cause of dislike, hatred and division, it were better to be without it, and to withdraw from such a religion would be a truly religious act. For it is clear that the purpose of a remedy is to cure; but if the remedy should only aggravate the complaint it had better be left alone. Any religion which is not a cause of love and unity is no religion. All the holy prophets were as doctors to the soul: they gave prescriptions for the healing of mankind; thus any remedy that causes disease does not come from the great and supreme Physician." ('Abdu'l-Bahá, *Paris Talks*, p. 130)

Bahá'u'lláh described true religion saying it is, "… a radiant light and an impregnable stronghold for the protection and welfare of the peoples of the world." (*Tablets of Bahá'u'lláh*, p. 252)

Bahá'u'lláh warned, "Should the lamp of religion be obscured, chaos and confusion will ensue, and the lights of fairness, of justice, of tranquility and peace cease to shine." (*Tablets of Bahá'u'lláh*, p. 125)

What is the Covenant?

Have you ever wondered why there are so many sects or denominations of the world's major religions? No wonder people are confused and disillusioned about what denomination to belong to and what to believe. This is not God's doing, but rather humanity's. Let's first look at what the term Covenant means. The Universal House of Justice explains:

> "A Covenant in the religious sense is a binding agreement between God and man, whereby God requires of man certain behaviour in return for which He guarantees certain blessings or whereby He gives man certain bounties in return for which He takes from those who accept them an undertaking to behave in a certain way." (*The Compilation of Compilations,* Vol. 1, p. 111)

Discussing the purpose of the Covenant, 'Abdu'l-Bahá states:

> "To ensure the unity and agreement He has entered into a Covenant with all the people of the world, including the interpreter and explainer of His teachings, so that no one may interpret or explain the religion of God according to his own view or opinion and thus create a sect founded upon his individual understanding of the divine Words." (*Promulgation of Universal Peace*, p. 456)

We are fortunate as Bahá'ís to have the Lesser Covenant, and because of it there will only ever be one Bahá'í Faith. Discussing the Lesser Covenant, the Universal House of Justice states:

> "There is also the Lesser Covenant that a Manifestation of God makes with His followers that they will accept His appointed successor after Him. If they do so, the Faith can remain united and pure. If not, the Faith becomes divided and its forces spent. It is a Covenant of this kind that Bahá'u'lláh made with His followers regarding 'Abdu'l-Bahá and that 'Abdu'l-

Bahá perpetuated through the Administrative Order ..."
(The Compilation of Compilations, Vol. 1, p. 111)

'Abdu'l-Bahá explains the unifying power of the Covenant:

"Were it not for the protecting power of the Covenant to guard the impregnable fort of the Cause of God, there would arise among the Bahá'ís, in one day, a thousand different sects as was the case in former ages. But in this Blessed Dispensation, for the sake of the permanency of the Cause of God and avoidance of dissension amongst the people of God, the Blessed Beauty, has through the Supreme Pen written the Covenant and the Testament; He appointed a Centre, the Exponent of the Book and the **annuller** of disputes. Whatever is written or said by Him is conformable truth and under the protection of the Blessed Beauty. He is infallible. The express purpose of this last Will and Testament is to set aside disputes from the world." *(Bahá'í World Faith*, pp. 357–358)

How does a person become a Bahá'í?

A person who recognises and acknowledges Bahá'u'lláh as the Manifestation of God for today, if they are 15 years of age or older, they may declare themselves a Bahá'í. The Universal House of Justice expands on this and states:

> "The prime motive should always be the response of man to God's Message, and the recognition of His Messenger. Those who declare themselves as Bahá'ís should become enchanted with the beauty of the teachings, and touched by the love of Bahá'u'lláh. The declarants need not know all the proofs, history, laws, and principles of the Faith, but in the process of declaring themselves they must, in addition to catching the spark of faith, become basically informed about the Central Figures of the Faith, as well as the existence of laws they must follow and an administration they must obey." (*Wellspring of Guidance*, p.32)

Sometimes when a person declares, they are asked to sign a declaration card; this is purely for administrative purposes. A couple of extracts have been provided taken from letters written on behalf of Shoghi Effendi to individual believers about when a person declares their faith in Bahá'u'lláh:

> "There is a difference between character and faith; it is often very hard to accept this fact and put up with it, but the fact remains that a person may believe in and love the Cause — even to be ready to die for it — and yet not have a good personal character or possess traits at **variance** with the teachings. We should try to change, to let the Power of God help recreate us and make us true Bahá'ís in deed as well as in belief. But sometimes the process is slow, sometimes it never happens because the individual does not try hard enough. But these things cause us suffering and are a test

to us in our fellow-believers, most, especially if we love them and have been their teachers!"

The process of becoming a Bahá'í is necessarily slow and gradual. The essential is not that the beginner should have a full and detailed knowledge of the Cause, a thing which is obviously impossible in the vast majority of cases, but that he should, by an act of his own will, be willing to uphold and follow the truth and guidance set forth in the Teachings, and thus open his heart and mind to the reality of the Manifestation." (Universal House of Justice, *Lights*, No. 264, pp. 75–76)

Why do we have 19 Days Feasts?

Every religion establishes its own calendar. The Bahá'í calendar is comprised of 19 months which each have 19 days. The remaining 4 days are known as Intercalary Days. The first day of the month is when Nineteen Day Feasts are held any time from sunset until sunset the following day. Nineteen Day Feasts have three components, the devotional, the administrative and social part. Depending on the size of the community these may be held in a Bahá'í centre, a hired hall, or in one of the community members' homes. Shoghi Effendi states the following about the three parts of the Nineteen Day Feast:

> "The significance of the Nineteen Day Feast is thus threefold. It is a gathering of a devotional, social and administrative importance. When these three features are all combined, this Feast can and will surely yield the best and the maximum of results. The friends, however, should be on their guard lest they overstress the significance of this institution created by Bahá'u'lláh. They should also take care not to underrate or minimise its importance." (*Compilation*, Vol. 1, p. 434)

Discussing the uniqueness of the Nineteen Day Feast Shoghi Effendi states:

> "... it is not only in the sense of its gradual unfoldment as an institution that the evolution of the Feast must be regarded; there is a broader context yet. The Feast may well be seen in its unique combination of modes as the culmination of a great historic process in which primary elements of community life — acts of worship, of festivity and other forms of togetherness — over vast stretches of time have achieved a glorious convergence. The Nineteen Day Feats represents the new stage in this enlightened age to which the basic expression of community life has evolved. Shoghi Effendi has

described it as the foundation of the new World Order ..."
(*The Compilations of Compilations*, Vol. 1, p. 420)

The Universal House of Justice reiterates the significance of the Nineteen Day Feasts and explains:

"The World Order of Bahá'u'lláh encompasses all units of human society; integrates the spiritual, administrative and social processes of life; and canalises human expression in its varied forms towards the construction of a new civilisation. The Nineteen Day Feast embraces all these aspects at the very base of society. Functioning in the village, the town, the city, it is an institution of which all the people of the Bahá are members. It is intended to promote unity, ensure progress, and foster joy." (*Messages from the Universal House of Justice 1986–2001*, pp. 132–33)

'Abdu'l-Bahá highlights how Bahá'ís will feel after attending a Nineteen Day Feast and states, "If this feast be held in the proper fashion, the friends will, once in nineteen days, find themselves spiritually restored, and endued with a power that is not of this world." (*Selections From the Writings of 'Abdu'l-Bahá*, p. 91)

Why can't Bahá'ís become involved in politics?

The news and social media are full of reports and opinions about partisan politics. Instead of working together in unity, our current political system is divided into opposing parties who are polarised from one another causing further divisions, factions, and disunity. Those involved in politics are forced to align themselves with a particular party whether they agree with all their decisions or not. The Bahá'í Community is working towards unity; therefore, Bahá'ís cannot become involved in politics. Below are several extracts taken from a message written by the Universal House of Justice stating:

> "The Faith of God is the sole source of salvation for mankind today. The true cause of the ills of humanity is its disunity. No matter how perfect may be the machinery devised by the leaders of men for the political unity of the world, it will still not provide the antidote to the poison sapping the vigour of present day society. These ills can be cured only through the instrumentality of God's Faith. There are many well-wishers of mankind who devote their efforts to relief work and charity and to the material well-being of man, but only Bahá'ís can do the work which God most wants done. When we devote ourselves to the work of the Faith, we are doing a work which is the greatest aid and only refuge for a needy and divided world.
>
> The Bahá'í Community is a world-wide organisation seeking to establish true and universal peace on earth. If a Bahá'í works for one political party to overcome another it is a negation of the very spirit of the Faith. Membership in any political party, therefore, necessarily entails repudiation of some or all of the principles of peace and unity proclaimed

by Bahá'u'lláh. As 'Abdu'l-Bahá stated: 'Our party is God's party — we don't belong to any party.'

If a Bahá'í were to insist on his right to support a certain political party, he could not deny the same degree of freedom to other believers. This would mean that within the ranks of the Faith, whose primary mission is to unite all men as one great family under God, there would be Bahá'ís opposed to each other. Where, then, would be the example of unity and harmony which the world is seeking?" (*Universal House of Justice, Messages 1963–1986*, pp. 163–165)

What Bahá'í book contains the laws of the Faith?

The *Kitáb-i-Aqdas* translated into English means *The Most Holy Book*. It is Bahá'u'lláh's book of laws and was written around 1873. In the introduction of the *Kitáb-i-Aqdas* the Universal House of Justice states:

> "'To build anew the whole world' is the claim and challenge of His Message, and the *Kitáb-i-Aqdas* is the Charter of the future world civilisation that Bahá'u'lláh has come to raise up. Its provisions rest squarely on the foundation established by past religions, for, in the words of Bahá'u'lláh, *'This is the changeless Faith of God, eternal in the past, eternal in the future'.* In this Revelation the concepts of the past are brought to a new level of understanding, and the social laws, changed to suit the age now dawning, are designed to carry humanity forward into a world civilisation the splendours of which can as yet be scarcely imagined.
>
> In its affirmation of the validity of the great religions of the past, the *Kitáb-i-Aqdas* reiterates those eternal truths **enunciated** by all the Divine Messengers: the unity of God, love of one's neighbour, and the moral purpose of earthly life. At the same time it removes those elements of past religious codes that now constitute obstacles to the emerging unification of the world and the reconstruction of human society.
>
> The Law of God for this Dispensation addresses the needs of the entire human family. There are laws in the *Kitáb-i-Aqdas* which are directed primarily to the members of a specific section of humanity and can be immediately understood by them but which, at first reading, may be obscure to people of a different culture.

Bahá'u'lláh asserts, 'Think not, that We have revealed unto you a mere code of laws. Nay, rather, We have unsealed the choice Wine with the fingers of might and power.'" (*The Kitáb-i-Aqdas,* pp. 1–3)

What is the Right of God (Huqúqu"lláh)?

Huqúqu"lláh is an Arabic word that means the Right of God. Huqúqu"lláh is one of the most sacred and important laws of Bahá'u'lláh, revealed in the Kitáb-i-Aqdas. It is the payment of part of a person's wealth after their living expenses and needs. This money is paid directly to the Universal House of Justice. The following quote by 'Abdu'l-Bahá explains what the money is spent on:

> "Thus every true and sincere believer will offer Huqúq to be expended for the relief of the poor, the disabled, the needy, and the orphans, and for other vital needs of the Cause of God, even as Christ did establish a Fund for benevolent purposes." (*The Compilation of Compilations* Vol. 1, p. 513)

The Universal House of Justice further elaborates in a letter to an individual believer on the use of Huqúqu"lláh and states, "… the use of funds from Huqúqu"lláh … entails a wide range of applications that will eventually address various needs of society in ways that will also contribute toward the solution of economic problems." (*Compilation on Huqúqu"lláh*, No.111)

With regards to what portion of a person's wealth is required to be paid, Bahá'u'lláh states, "Should anyone acquire one hundred mithqals of gold, nineteen mithqals thereof are God's and to be rendered unto Him." (*Kitáb-i-Aqdas*: K 97, p. 55)

What is a mithqal of gold you ask? A mithqal is an ancient Arabic unit used to measure precious metals, no longer used. A mithqal of gold is 4.25 grams of gold.

Payment of Huqúqu"lláh should be viewed as a blessing and privilege. With regards as to one's attitude when paying Huqúq, Bahá'u'lláh states, "Should anyone offer Huqúq with utmost joy and radiance, manifesting a spirit of resignation and content, his offering shall be acceptable before God …" (*Huqúqu"lláh – The Right of God*, p. 6)

What is the Lesser Peace?

Bahá'u'lláh's main mission in coming during this time in history is to bring about the oneness of humanity and peace among the world's nations. Peace will come in stages, the first of which will be the Lesser Peace. The Lesser Peace is defined in the following extracts from a letter written on behalf of the Universal House of Justice:

"First, there will come the Lesser Peace, when the unity of nations will be achieved, then gradually the Most Great Peace — the spiritual as well as social and political unity of mankind, when the Bahá'í World Commonwealth, operating in strict accordance with the laws and ordinances of the Most Holy Book of the Bahá'í Revelation, will have been established through the efforts of the Bahá'ís.

As to the Lesser Peace, Shoghi Effendi has explained that this will initially be a political unity arrived at by decision of the governments of various nations; it will not be established by direct action of the Bahá'í community. This does not mean, however, that the Bahá'ís are standing aside and waiting for the Lesser Peace to come before they do something about the peace of mankind. Indeed, by promoting the principles of the Faith, which are indispensable to the maintenance of peace, and by fashioning the instruments of the Bahá'í Administrative Order, which we are told by the beloved Guardian is the pattern for future society, the Bahá'ís are constantly engaged in laying the groundwork for a permanent peace, the Most Great Peace being their ultimate goal." (*The Compilation of Compilations, Vol. 2*, pp. 199–200)

Tahirih Lemon

Glossary

Abasement: the action or fact of abasing or being abased; humiliation or degradation.

Admonishing: warn or reprimand someone firmly.

Aliments: food; nourishment.

Ameliorated: make something bad or unsatisfactory better.

Annuller: one that declare invalid an official agreement, decision, or result.

Axiomatic: self-evident or unquestionable.

Circumscribed: restrict something within limits.

Complements: a thing that contributes extra features to something else in such a way as to improve or emphasise its quality.

Doctrines: a belief or set of beliefs held and taught by a Church, political party, or other group.

Efficacy: the ability to produce a desired or intended result.

Emanate: a feeling, quality, or sensation issue or spread out from a source.

Embodiment: a tangible or visible form of an idea, quality, or feeling.

Endowed: provide with a quality, ability, or asset.

Enunciated: express a proposition, theory in clear or definite terms.

Incumbent: necessary for someone as a duty or responsibility.

Intermediary: a person who acts as a link between people in order to try and bring about an agreement; a mediator.

Partisanship: prejudice in favour of a particular cause; bias.

Permissive: allowing or characterised by great or excessive freedom or behaviour.

Preeminent: surpassing all others; very distinguished in some way.

Promptings: the actions of saying something to persuade, encourage, or remind someone to do or say something.

Purgation: purification or cleansing.

Stipulate: demand or specify a requirement, typically as part of an agreement.

Variance: the fact or quality of being different, divergent, or inconsistent.

Vicissitudes: a change of circumstances or fortune, typically one that is unwelcome or unpleasant.

BIBLIOGRAPHY

'Abdu'l-Bahá and Mírzá Mahmúd-i-Zarqání, *Mahmúd's Diary: The Diary of Mírzá Mahmúd-i-Zarqání Chronicling 'Abdu'l-Bahá's Journey to America.* George Ronald: Oxford, England, 1998.

'Abdu'l-Bahá, *Paris Talks.* Bahá'í Publishing Trust, London, England, 1972.

'Abdu'l-Bahá, *The Promulgation of Universal Peace.* Bahá'í Publishing Trust, Wilmette, IL, 1982.

'Abdu'l-Bahá, *Selections from the Writings of 'Abdu'l-Bahá.* Bahá'í World Centre, Haifa, Israel, 1978.

'Abdu'l-Bahá, *Some Answered Questions.* Bahá'í Publishing Trust, Wilmette, IL, 1991.

'Abdu'l-Bahá, *Tablet to Auguste Forel.* The Bahá'í World, Vol. XV, Bahá'í World Centre, Haifa, Israel, 1976.

Bahá'í Prayers and Tablets for the Young. Bahá'í Publishing Trust, Wilmette, IL, 1978.

Bahá'í World Faith. Bahá'í Publishing Trust Wilmette, IL, 1976.

Bahá'u'lláh, *Epistle to The Son of the Wolf.* Bahá'í Publishing Trust, Wilmette, IL,1988.

Bahá'u'lláh, *The Hidden Words of Bahá'u'lláh.* Carmel Publishers, New Delhi, India, 2022.

Bahá'u'lláh, *Glad Tidings Tablets of Bahá'u'lláh Revealed After the Kitáb-i-Aqdas.* (Pocket Edition) US Bahá'í Publishing Trust, Wilmette, IL, 1988.

Bahá'u'lláh, *Gleanings from The Writings of Bahá'u'lláh.* Bahá'í Publishing Trust, Wilmette, IL, 1983.

Bahá'u'lláh, *Kitáb-i-Aqdas.* Bahá'í Publications Australia, Torquay, VIC, 1993.

Compilation of Compilations, Vol. 1. Bahá'í Publications Australia, Maryborough, VIC, 1991.

Compilation of Compilations, Vol. 2. Bahá'í Publications Australia, Maryborough, VIC, 1991.

Holley, Horace, *Bahá'í Scriptures.* (2nd Edition), Bahá'í Publishing Committee, New York, NY, USA, 1928.

Hornby, Hellen, *Light of Guidance A Bahá'í Reference File.* (2nd Edition), Bahá'í Publishing Trust, New Delhi, India, 1988.

J.E. Esslemont, *Bahá'u'lláh and The New Era.* US Bahá'í Publishing Trust, Wilmette, IL,1980.

Shoghi Effendi, *Dawn of a New Day: Messages to India, 1923–1957.* New Delhi, India, Bahá'í Publishing Trust,1970.

Shoghi Effendi, *Directives from The Guardian.* New Delhi, India, 1973.

Shoghi Effendi, *Light of Divine Guidance: The Messages from the Guardian of the Bahá'í of Germany and Austria.* Vol. II, Hofheim-Langenhain: Bahá'í-Verlag, 1985.

Shoghi Effendi, *Unfolding Destiny: The Messages from the Guardian of the Bahá'í Faith to the Bahá'í Community of the British Isles.* Bahá'í Publishing Trust, London, England, 1981.

Universal House of Justice, *Messages from the Universal House of Justice 1986-2001.* Bahá'í Publishing Trust, Wilmette, IL, 2009.

Universal House of Justice, Wellspring of Guidance: Messages from the Universal House of Justice 1963-1968. Bahá'í Publishing Trust, Wilmette, IL, 1969.

Various Authors, *Huqúqu"lláh –The Right of God.* Compiled by the Research Department of the Universal House of Justice, Bahá'í World Centre, April 2007.

https://aifs.gov.au/cfca/publications/physical-punishment-legislation

https://www.alzint.org/about/dementia-facts-figures/dementia-statistics/

https://bahai-library.com/abdul-baha_divine_philosophy

https://www.bahai.org/library/authoritative-texts/compilations/huququllah-right-god/1#925886939

https://bahai-library.com/hornby_lights_guidance&chapter=all#nnnXXIV.B

https://bahai-library.com/compilations/bahai.scriptures/8.html

https://bahai-library.com/compilation_compilations_1

https://bahai-library.com/compilation_economics_agriculture#s4

https://bahai-library.com/compilation_spiritualism_reincarnation

https://bahai-library.com/compilation_youth

https://bahai-library.com/uhj_five-year_plan_2011

https://www.britannica.com/topic/Christmas

https://www.britannica.com/topic/miracle

https://www.dementia.org.au/about-dementia/what-is-dementia

https://www.healthdirect.gov.au/abortion

https://kidshelpline.com.au/teens/issues/bullying

https://languages.oup.com/research/oxford-english-dictionary/

https://www.un.org/en/climatechange/science/key-findings#physical-science

http://mhaustralia.org/resources/frequently-asked-questions/what-mental-illness

https://www.who.int/emergencies/diseases/novel-coronavirus-2019/advice-for-public/myth-busters